Dedication

To Zoe, Victoria, Laura, Sydney, Khalis, Nailah, Brittney,
Vashti, Jöhann, Adam, Mina, Antar, and Omar
in hopes that you follow your own dreams.

In loving memory of
my brother, Charles George Hicks (1963–2004),
and cousin, Anita Hunter Cole (1960–2005).

—KEH

Martha Ann's Quilt for Queen Victoria

Manufactured in China.

 For information, please contact:
Brown Books Publishing Group
16200 North Dallas Parkway, Suite 170
Dallas, Texas 75248
www.brownbooks.com
972-381-0009
A New Era in Publishing™

ISBN-13: 978-1-933285-59-7   ISBN-10: 1-933285-59-1   LCCN: 2006906822
1 2 3 4 5 6 7 8 9 10

FIRST EDITION

Library of Congress Cataloging-in-Publication Data
Hicks, Kyra E., 1965—Martha Ann's Quilt for Queen Victoria / written by Kyra E. Hicks; illustrated by
Lee Edward Födi. 1st ed.
p. cm. ISBN-13: 978-1-933285-59-7
1. Ricks, Martha Ann, b. ca. 1817—Juvenile literature. 2. African American women—Liberia—Biography—Juvenile literature. 3. African Americans—Liberia—Biography—Juvenile literature. 4. Slaves—Tennessee, East—Biography—Juvenile literature. 5. Quilts—Liberia—History—19th century—Juvenile literature. 6. Quilts—England—History—19th century—Juvenile literature. 7. Victoria, Queen of Great Britain, 1819–1901—Juvenile literature. 8. Liberia—Biography—Juvenile literature. 9. Tennessee, East—Biography—Juvenile literature. I. Födi, Lee Edward, ill. II. Title.
DT633.3.R53H53 2006
305.896'073006662092—dc22
[B]
2006024651

Martha Ann's
Quilt
for
Queen Victoria

Written by
Kyra E. Hicks

Illustrated by
Lee Edward Födi

To: Roland Freeman
Thank you for all
your encouragement over
the years!
Love,
Kyra Hicks
11/2006

Martha Ann loved one chore most. Her special job was to place Papa's money in his old, red tin box. Martha Ann was a slave. Her papa, George Erskine, was a free man and traveling preacher. Each Sunday the congregation would take up a collection after Papa's sermons to help him raise money for his family's freedom. When Papa came home, Mama counted the money, and Martha Ann dropped the dollars and coins in the old, red tin box.

Martha Ann was born about 1817 on the Doherty Plantation in eastern Tennessee. Slaves worked long, backbreaking hours there without pay. Slave children weren't allowed to go to school.

Martha Ann's brothers, Wallace and Weir, worked in the fields. Her older sisters, Jane and Mary, helped Mama with the household chores. Martha Ann helped Grandma babysit Hopkins and Sarah, her younger brother and sister.

One Sunday, Papa raced home excited because he had learned about the American Colonization Society, a group that helped blacks start a new life in Africa—in a place called Liberia.

"Children in Liberia attend school," Papa told the family.

"Could I go to school and learn to read, Papa?" Martha Ann asked.

"Yes, you can." Papa said. "You'll make us proud."

Martha Ann was now more eager than ever to see the money in the old, red tin box grow.

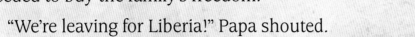

Martha Ann was twelve when Papa finally saved $2,400, the amount needed to buy the family's freedom.

"We're leaving for Liberia!" Papa shouted.

Martha Ann danced with excitement.

"I'm going to school!"

Martha Ann and her family sailed to Liberia in 1830. The American Colonization Society provided Papa with land on which he and the boys built a house and planted crops.

School was open to all children in Liberia. For the first time, Martha Ann sat in a real classroom and eagerly learned to read.

At home, Mama taught Martha Ann and her sisters to cut fabric, thread a needle, and sew straight, even stitches. Mama even taught the girls to sew clothes and stitch quilts.

"Mama, one day I'll be as good as you with my needle and thread!" Martha Ann declared.

"Yes, you will," Mama said. "You'll make us proud."

But bad times soon came. *African fever* swept through town. Papa, Mama, and Martha Ann's sisters died of the fever. Even Grandma and Weir died. Martha Ann cried and cried for many days because she missed them all very much. Wallace, her oldest brother, wrapped Martha Ann and Hopkins in his arms.

"Do you want to return to America?" Wallace asked.

"No," she trembled. "I want to stay here and go to school. I want Papa and Mama to be proud of me."

Martha Ann grew up and married Sion Harris. One evening, she read in the *Liberian Herald* about Victoria, the new queen of England. Martha Ann thought the queen looked lovely.

Martha Ann walked with Sion to the market each week. She watched British naval ships patrolling the coast of Liberia to stop slave catchers from kidnapping black folks and forcing them into slavery. Martha Ann *never* wanted to be a slave again and work long, hard hours without pay. She admired Queen Victoria for trying to save her and others from slavery by sending the navy.

"Sion, I know how I can make Papa and Mama proud of me!" she announced. "Queen Victoria is a true friend to our people. I want to thank her for being so kind and protecting us. I'll thank the queen in person!"

"In person?" said an astonished Sion. "England is 3,500 miles away. How will you get there or meet the queen?"

"I'll find a way," she promised.

Martha Ann remembered how Papa saved money to buy the family's freedom. That evening, she found Papa's old, red tin box and placed a few spare coins into it for her trip to see Queen Victoria.

Martha Ann taught at the local mission where Sion worked too.

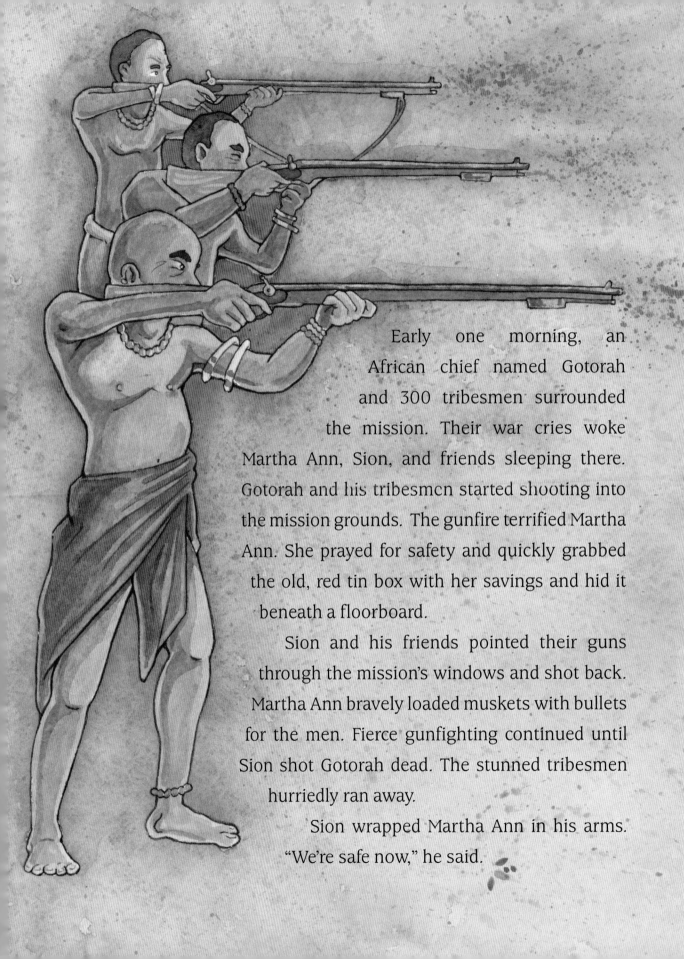

Early one morning, an African chief named Gotorah and 300 tribesmen surrounded the mission. Their war cries woke Martha Ann, Sion, and friends sleeping there. Gotorah and his tribesmen started shooting into the mission grounds. The gunfire terrified Martha Ann. She prayed for safety and quickly grabbed the old, red tin box with her savings and hid it beneath a floorboard.

Sion and his friends pointed their guns through the mission's windows and shot back. Martha Ann bravely loaded muskets with bullets for the men. Fierce gunfighting continued until Sion shot Gotorah dead. The stunned tribesmen hurriedly ran away.

Sion wrapped Martha Ann in his arms. "We're safe now," he said.

Sion and Martha Ann moved from the mission to their own farm. They sold vegetables at the market. Martha Ann continued to save her spare coins in the old, red tin box.

Martha Ann cried when Sion died unexpectedly. She lived alone for many years until she met and married Henry Ricks, a widower with three sons. Henry had a farm in the town of Clay-Ashland where he grew coffee, ginger, and cotton.

Martha Ann wove cloth from Henry's cotton. She sewed clothes for her new family as well as for pay. She was now as good as Mama with a needle and thread. Martha Ann continued to drop spare coins into the old, red tin box.

"Martha Ann, when are you off to see Queen Victoria?" laughed Henry. "You don't even have a gift for her!"

Henry's laughter hurt Martha Ann. Henry loved Martha Ann, but he couldn't imagine her ever meeting the queen.

"Henry, I admire Queen Victoria for her kindness. You'll see," Martha Ann said determinedly. "One day I'll thank her in person, and I *will* have a gift."

Martha Ann spent weeks thinking about a suitable gift for the queen. She decided to sew a beautiful quilt just as Mama taught her. She looked out onto the farm and selected one of Henry's coffee trees for the design. Each night she sewed pieces of cloth together for the quilt.

The townspeople knew about Martha Ann's dream to visit Queen Victoria and of the quilt she was sewing. The grown-ups laughed at her. The children jumped rope and teasingly sang:

"Auntie Martha gonna see the Queen,
Stitching a quilt of coffee beans.
How many stitches will it take?
Two–four–six–eight!"

Many years passed. Henry died of old age. Martha Ann was now an old woman and determined as ever to make Papa and Mama proud. Martha Ann counted the money in Papa's old, red tin box. "Hallelujah!" she shouted. Finally, she had enough to pay for her trip to England.

"But how will I ever meet the queen?" she asked herself.

One afternoon, Martha Ann received an unexpected visitor—Mrs. Jane Roberts, the wife of Liberia's first president, Joseph J. Roberts.

"I've heard you're making a fancy quilt for Queen Victoria. May I see it?" Mrs. Roberts asked.

Martha Ann unfolded the quilt, which had hundreds of green leaves and dozens of plump, red coffee beans made of fabric.

"It's exquisite!" Mrs. Roberts said. "I'll help you meet Queen Victoria."

Mrs. Roberts wrote to Dr. Edward Blyden, the Liberian ambassador in London, and asked him to help Martha Ann meet the queen. Dr. Blyden quickly agreed.

After years of teasing Martha Ann and laughing at her impossible dream, the townspeople watched in amazement as 76-year-old Martha Ann, holding her quilt, boarded a ship to England.

Dr. Blyden wrote to Queen Victoria, requesting an audience. *The London Times* even published an article about Martha Ann saving her pennies for fifty years for her trip to see the queen. The British people rallied for Martha Ann.

Soon a telegram arrived.

"By command of Her Majesty,

Mrs. Martha Ann Ricks and guests

are invited to a reception at

Windsor Castle on

Saturday the 16th of July 1892."

The day Martha Ann dreamed of finally came! She stood expectantly
in a great room when a nearby door opened. Victoria, Queen of Great
Britain and Empress of India, entered. Then, to Martha Ann's surprise,

the queen's son, Prince Edward, and his family followed.

"I feel greatly honored by the trouble you have taken to visit with me," said Queen Victoria.

Martha Ann curtsied and shook hands with the queen.

"Your Majesty, you're a great friend to my people," Martha Ann said. "I don't have much, but I hope you'll cherish this gift." Two servants unfolded the *Coffee Tree* quilt.

"It's most beautiful!" Queen Victoria declared.

"A splendid creation indeed," Prince Edward agreed.

"Tell me about your life as a slave in America and of your freedom in Liberia," requested the queen. The two women talked together until the Royal Family had to leave.

"Thank you for the lovely quilt," Queen Victoria said. "You're quite skilled with a needle and thread."

The townspeople cheered and waved flags when Martha Ann returned to Liberia. A marching band played welcoming songs. Martha Ann was now greeted as a heroine by those who once laughed at her.